The National Archives

PC 29 (46-17)
December 1945

RECORD GROUP NO. 153: RECORDS OF THE OFFICE OF THE JUDGE ADVOCATE GENERAL (WAR)

Preliminary Checklist

of the

Records of the Office

of the

Judge Advocate General (War)

1808–1942:
Record Group 153, PC 29

Compiled by

George J. Stansfield
War Records Office

Heritage Books
2024

HERITAGE BOOKS

AN IMPRINT OF HERITAGE BOOKS, INC.

Books, CDs, and more—Worldwide

For our listing of thousands of titles see our website
at
www.HeritageBooks.com

A Facsimile Reprint
Published 2024 by
HERITAGE BOOKS, INC.
Publishing Division
5810 Ruatan Street
Berwyn Heights, MD 20740

National Archives Library
January 14 1946

International Standard Book Number
Paperbound: 978-0-7884-5771-5

CONTENTS

Page

INTRODUCTION

The Judge Advocate General's Department was established by an act of Congress of July 5, 1884, which consolidated the Bureau of Military Justice, with the Judge Advocate General as its head, and the corps of judge advocates of the Army. Although this act marked the formal establishment of the present department (which is headed by the Office of the Judge Advocate General), there had been a judge advocate of the Continental Army as early as 1775, and provision had been made by law for a judge advocate within the Army in 1797. The number and status of judge advocates varied during the next 50 years. In 1849 provision was made for the appointment of a Judge Advocate of the Army; and this officer was designated as the Judge Advocate General by an act of July 17, 1862, which provided also that all records of courts martial and of military commissions be forwarded to him. Prior to that date those records were kept in the Office of the Secretary of War until 1835 and after that in the Office of the Adjutant General. The act further provided that each army in the field should have a judge advocate.

In 1864 the Judge Advocate General was placed at the head of the newly created Bureau of Military Justice, the function of which was to administer justice in the Army. The act of 1884 that changed the status of the Bureau by providing for the Judge Advocate General's Department did not change its powers and duties, and today the Judge Advocate General is still the chief legal adviser of the War Department and the Army and is in charge of the system of military justice. The functions of his Office include the furnishing of advice on the legal phases of the business, property, and financial operations under the Secretary of War and on legal questions concerning the administration, control, discipline, and civil relations of the personnel of the Army. On March 9, 1942, the Judge Advocate General was brought under the direct command of the Commanding General, Services of Supply, except for his functions in regard to court martial and certain legal matters concerning which he reports directly to the Secretary of War.

The records of the Office of the Judge Advocate General in the National Archives that are included in this record group and described in this preliminary checklist consist of the central correspondence files, 1842-1912; records relating to the administration of military justice, including general court-martial case files, 1808-1938, and the revision of the court-martial manual, 1918-28; records of certain investigations undertaken by the Office, 1864-1927; records relating to personnel, 1877-1923; and certain international claims files involving Mexico and the Netherlands, 1914-40. Also included are the records of the Assistant Judge Advocate General, 1864-67, and of the Acting Judge Advocate General in Europe, 1918-19.

Records created or inherited by units within the Office of the Judge Advocate General include those of the Military Reservation Division, 1808-1942, relating to military reservations no longer in the possession of the War Department; those of the Civil Affairs Section and the Litigation

Division, 1921-42, relating principally to cases tried in the United States Court of Claims; minutes of meetings and correspondence of the War Transactions Board, 1923-26; and records of the Insular Affairs Section, 1915-39, consisting of correspondence, legal opinions, and case files relating to matters involving the War Department and residents of insular possessions of the United States, notably the Philippines and Puerto Rico.

The patent records described in this checklist were created in the Central Patent Section of the Judge Advocate General's Department, its predecessor agencies, and patent commissions on which members of the Section served. Among the commissions whose records are represented in this record group are the Commission on the Adjustment of Foreign Claims, 1922-24, and the Commission for the Adjustment of British Claims, 1932-33. Also included are the records dealing with the investigatory activities of the Section in the settlement of German-Austrian claims, 1928-33. Other records included are those of such predecessor and ancillary patent boards as the Interdepartmental Patents Board, 1922-26; the Munitions Patent Board, 1918-21; the Patent Section of the Purchase Branch of the Purchase, Storage, and Traffic Division, War Department General Staff, 1919-21; and the Patents Branch of the Procurement Division, Office of the Chief of Ordnance, 1918-19.

The records covered by this preliminary checklist amount to 4,532 cubic feet and were transferred to the National Archives as Accessions 928 (pt.), 1409, 1438, 1457, 1923, 1924, and 2031. Other records for the same period are in the Office of the Judge Advocate General and in the War Department Records Branch, The Adjutant General's Office.

Judge Advocates, 1775-1945

Name and title	Period of service
William Tudor, Judge Advocate of the Army	July 29, 1775-Aug. 9, 1776
Lt. Col. William Tudor, Judge Advocate General	Aug. 10, 1776-Apr. 9, 1777
Lt. Col. John Lawrence, Judge Advocate	Apr. 10, 1777-June 3, 1782
Lt. Col. James Innis, " "	July 9-Sept. 12, 1782
Maj. Richard Howell, " "	Sept. 18-Oct. 1, 1782
Lt. Thomas Edwards, " "	Oct. 2, 1782-Nov. 3, 1783
Lt. Campbell Smith, " "	July 16, 1794-July 13, 1796
Capt. Campbell Smith, " "	June 2, 1797-June 1, 1802
Maj. Thomas Gales, " "	Sept. 26, 1812-Dec. 16, 1814
Maj. E. A. Bancker, " "	Mar. 18, 1813-June 15, 1815
Maj. J. S. Wills, " "	May 7, 1813-June 15, 1815
Maj. J. T. Dent, " "	July 19, 1813-Apr. 14, 1818
Maj. Stephen Lush, Jr., " "	Oct. 5, 1813-June 15, 1815
Maj. R. H. Winder, " "	July 9, 1814-June 15, 1815
Maj. Henry Wheaton, " "	Aug. 6, 1814-May 9, 1816
Maj. L. M. Parker, " "	Sept. 16, 1814-June 15, 1815
Maj. Samuel Wilcocks, " "	Dec. 19, 1814-June 15, 1815
Maj. W. O. Winston, " "	Apr. 29, 1816-Apr. 14, 1818
Maj. Thomas Hanson, " "	Apr. 29, 1816-Apr. 14, 1818
Maj. R. G. Winder, " "	May 3, 1816-July 23, 1818
Maj. S. A. Storrow, " "	July 9, 1816-June 1, 1821
Maj. J. L. Leib, " "	July 9, 1816-Jan. 15, 1817
Maj. C. D. Hays, " "	Sept. 10, 1818-June 1, 1821
Bvt. Maj. J. F. Lee, Judge Advocate of the Army	Mar. 2, 1849-Sept. 4, 1862
Brig. Gen. Joseph Holt, Judge Advocate General	Sept. 3, 1862-Dec. 1, 1875
Brig. Gen. W. McK. Dunn, " " "	Dec. 1, 1875-Jan. 22, 1881
Brig. Gen. D. G. Swaim, " " "	Feb. 18, 1881-Dec. 22, 1894
Brig. Gen. G. N. Lieber, " " "	Jan. 3, 1895-May 21, 1901
Brig. Gen. T. F. Barr, " " "	May 21-May 22, 1901
Brig. Gen. J. W. Clous, " " "	May 22-May 24, 1901
Brig. Gen. G. B. Davis, " " "	May 24, 1901-Feb. 14, 1911
Brig. Gen. Enoch A. Crowder, " " "	Feb. 15, 1911-Oct. 9, 1917
Maj. Gen. Enoch A. Crowder, " " "	Oct. 10, 1917-Feb. 14, 1923
Maj. Gen. Walter A. Bethel, " " "	Feb. 15, 1923-Nov. 15, 1924
Maj. Gen. John A. Hull, " " "	Nov. 16, 1924-Nov. 15, 1928
Maj. Gen. Edward A. Kreger, " " "	Nov. 16, 1928-Mar. 5, 1931
Maj. Gen. Blanton Winship, " " "	Mar. 6, 1931-Nov. 30, 1933
Maj. Gen. Arthur W. Brown, " " "	Dec. 1, 1933-Nov. 30, 1937
Maj. Gen. Allen W. Gullion, " " "	Dec. 1, 1937-Nov. 30, 1941
Maj. Gen. Myron C. Cramer, " " "	Dec. 1, 1941-

CHECKLIST

RECORDS OF THE IMMEDIATE OFFICE OF THE JUDGE ADVOCATE GENERAL

Correspondence

LETTERS SENT ("Record Books"). 1842-89. 57 vols. 15 ft.   1
    Copies of letters sent by The Adjutant General, Acting Judge Advo-
cates, the Judge Advocate of the Army, and the Judge Advocate General
and reports to the Secretary of War, bureaus of the War Department,
Judge Advocates, other departments, Members of Congress, and others on
a wide variety of matters pertaining to military justice, including
the review of action taken by courts martial, military commissions,
and courts of inquiry; applications for pardon or mitigation of sentences; and the legal sufficiency of bonds and contracts given, made,
or accepted by the military authorities. Included also are copies of
opinions furnished from time to time upon the varied questions of law
submitted to the Office and of deeds, licenses, and other legal in-
struments prepared in the Office. Arranged chronologically. Name and
subject index in each volume. For separate indexes see following
entry.
    This series ends on February 21, 1889, and is continued in substance
in the press copies of letters sent, vol. 30, p. 312 (see entry 3).

INDEXES TO LETTERS SENT. 1842-76. 4 vols. 9 in.   2
    Volume 1 is a subject index; the other 3 volumes are name indexes.
Arranged alphabetically by initial letter of subject or correspondent's
name.

LETTERS SENT ("Record Copy Books"). 1882-95. 65 vols. 6 ft.   3
    Press copies of letters sent by the Judge Advocate General, similar
in content to those described in entry 1. Arranged chronologically.
Name and subject index in each volume. For separate index see entry 5.

LETTERS SENT ("Record Books"). 1889-95. 35 vols. 4 ft. 8 in.   4
    Typescript copies of selected letters sent by the Judge Advocate Gen-
eral as head of the system of military justice and as legal adviser to
the Secretary of War. These letters have been regarded as opinions of
the Judge Advocate General. They were copied from letters in volumes
30-65 of the press copy books described above. Arranged chronologically,
volumes numbered 30-65. Volume 30 contains letters copied from volumes
30 and 31; there is no volume 31 but there are two volumes numbered 32.
For index see entry 5.

INDEXES TO LETTERS SENT. 1882-95. 4 vols. 6 in.   5
    Name and subject indexes to the two series of letters sent described
in entries 3 and 4.

LETTERS RECEIVED. 1854-94. 7 ft. 6 in. <u>6</u>

Letters received by the Judge Advocate of the Army and the Judge
Advocate General, together with lists of records in this series that
were destroyed. For the period 1854 through 1870 the letters are arranged numerically, nos. 1-2579, in accordance with numbers assigned
in the registers described below; thereafter they are arranged by year
and numerically thereunder. For registers and indexes see the following entries.

REGISTERS OF LETTERS RECEIVED. 1854-89. 8 vols. 2 ft. <u>7</u>

Abstracts of letters received by the Judge Advocate of the Army and
the Judge Advocate General giving date of receipt, file number, name of
writer, date and purport of communication, and action taken. The first
volume in this series is erroneously numbered 100. Arranged chronologically by date of receipt except volumes for 1854-70, which are arranged
alphabetically and chronologically thereunder. Indexes in volumes for
1877-86. Separate indexes are described in the following entry.

INDEXES TO LETTERS RECEIVED. 1871-76, 1885-88. 3 vols. 6 in. <u>8</u>

Name and subject indexes to letters received and to three registers
of letters received (see entries above), arranged for each year alphabetically by initial letter of surname of writer or of subject.

DOCUMENT FILE. 1894-1912. 61 ft. <u>9</u>

Correspondence of the Office of the Judge Advocate General, consisting of press or carbon copies of letters sent, endorsements, and related
papers, and a relatively small number of letters received. Arranged
numerically, nos. 1-29,808. For record cards and index see following
entries.

RECORD CARDS. 1894-1912. 14 ft. <u>10</u>

Cards containing digests of communications received by the Judge
Advocate General and copies of memoranda, endorsements, opinions,
letters sent, and notations showing actions by the Office relating to
each subject. Arranged numerically, nos. 1-29,808. For index see
following entry.

INDEX TO DOCUMENT FILE. 1894-1912. 23 ft. <u>11</u>

Name and subject index cards, giving date and number of correspondence and of record cards described in entries above.

OPINIONS OF THE ATTORNEY GENERAL. 1821-70. 5 vols. 1 ft. <u>12</u>

Copies of opinions and decisions of the Attorney General, with a few
of the Secretary of War, concerning the administration of military
justice and the legal actions of the War Department. Arranged chronologically by date of opinion or decision. Name and subject index in
each volume.

OFFICE FILE OF MAJOR BACON. 1918-33. 1 ft. <u>13</u>

Correspondence, work papers, and personal papers of Maj. J. A. Bacon,
Judge Advocate General's Office, relating to maritime affairs (1918-23),
the trial of Maj. A. K. Tayloe (1928), and the Commission for Adjustment
of British Claims (1932-33). Arranged alphabetically by subject.

COURT-MARTIAL CASE FILES. 1808-15. 8 vols. 1 ft. 6 in.   14
    Copies of records of general courts martial and courts of inquiry.
Included are documents describing the organization and personnel of the
courts; charges and specifications; pleas and arraignments of the defendants; and proceedings, findings, and sentences of the courts. Volume 1 contains principally material concerning the court martial in 1815
of Gen. James Wilkinson. The second volume contains material concerning
a number of trials dating as early as 1808. There are two volumes numbered 4 for the period 1811-14. Arranged chronologically by date of
trial. Each volume contains a list of defendants arranged chronologically
by date of trial, which serves as an index.

COURT-MARTIAL CASE FILES. 1809-1938. 5,133 ft.   15
    Records of general courts martial, courts of inquiry, and military
commissions. Included are documents describing the organization and
personnel of the courts; charges and specifications; pleas and arraignments of the defendants; papers and exhibits submitted for the consid-
eration of the courts; proceedings, findings, and sentences of the courts;
reports of the reviewing authorities; statements of action by the Secretary of War and the President; and related correspondence. Arranged alphabetically by key letters arbitarily assigned the cases and numerically
thereunder (1809-94); arranged numerically by date of filing, nos.
1-211,959 (1894-1938). Prior to 1812 the records are fragmentary. The
papers for a few cases tried prior to 1938 have been retained in the Office of the Judge Advocate General.

REGISTERS OF COURT-MARTIAL CASES. 1809-90. 15 vols. 3 ft. 6 in.   16
    Lists of cases described above giving number of each; name, rank, and
organization of the defendant; names of the President of the court and
the Judge Advocate; and where and when the court was convened. Arranged
alphabetically by initial letter of surname of defendant. There are four
additional registers for the years 1862-68, arranged alphabetically by key
letters and thereunder by case number.

INDEX TO COURT-MARTIAL CASES. 1891-1917. 88 ft. 6 in.   17
    Card index to cases (see entry 15), giving name, rank, and organization
of defendant, War Department order announcing sentence, number of the case,
and date registered in the Office of the Judge Advocate General. Arranged
alphabetically by name of defendant. The index for the period from 1917
to date is in the Office of the Judge Advocate General.

COURT-MARTIAL CASE FILES. 1861-65. 3 ft. 9 in.   18
    Case files lost during the Civil War and recovered by the Judge Advo-
cate General in 1890 and 1891. The cases were not recorded in the registers described in entry 16. Arranged numerically, nos. 1-206.

LIST OF MISSING COURT-MARTIAL CASE FILES. 1860-70. 1 vol. 1 in.   19
    A list of cases for which the papers are missing from the series de-
scribed in entry 15, giving name of defendant, his organization, and the
case number. Arranged alphabetically by initial letter of surname of
defendant.

LIST OF COURT-MARTIAL CASE FILES WITHDRAWN AND NOT RETURNED. 1863-70.
    1 vol. 1 in.   20
    A list of case files (see entry 15) that were loaned to individuals
and not returned, giving case number; name, rank, and organization of
the accused; the date; and to whom the papers were loaned. These were
withdrawn from the series described in entry 15. In the same volume is
a list of cases not originally entered in the registers described in
entry 16. Arranged alphabetically by initial letter of surname of defendant.

LIST OF COURT-MARTIAL CASE FILES WITHDRAWN AND RETURNED. 1874-96.
    2 vols. 6 in.   21
    A list of case files withdrawn from court-martial files (see entry
15), giving case number; name, rank, and unit of individual concerned;
when the file was withdrawn and for whom; and when returned. Arranged
alphabetically by initial letter of surname of defendant, and chronologically thereunder.

COURT-MARTIAL ORDERS. 1810-24. 9 in.   22
    The orders are accompanied by supplementary correspondence and copies
of charges preferred against various officers and of proceedings of courts
martial. Arranged chronologically.

COURT-MARTIAL ORDERS. 1918-19. 4 ft.   23
    Copies of orders giving résumés of trials by general courts martial.
Arranged by organization.

CLEMENCY APPLICATIONS. 1887-38. 4 ft. 4 in.   24
    Applications for and correspondence regarding clemency for prisoners
sentenced by general courts martial to the United States Military Prison
at Fort Leavenworth, Kans. Arranged numerically by court-martial case
number (see entries 15 and 16).

CLEMENCY ORDERS. 1894-97. 1 vol. 1 in.   25
    Press copies of orders issued by Assistant Secretary of War Joseph B.
Doe with regard to the lessening of sentences or the pardon of individuals
convicted under military law. Arranged chronologically.

RECORDS RELATING TO REVISIONS OF THE COURT-MARTIAL MANUAL. 1919-27.
    9 ft. 6 in.   26
    Correspondence, work papers, and reports relating to various revisions
of the manual, together with copies of documents relating to the Ansell-
Baker controversy over court-martial sentences during the World War. Arranged chronologically.

REPORT ON CRITICISMS OF COURT-MARTIAL PROCEDURE. 1919. 1 binder.
    6 in.   27
    Report made by Maj. William C. Rigby to Gen. Enoch C. Crowder, Judge
Advocate General, dated February 13, 1919, relating to criticisms of the
system of military justice and containing descriptions of systems followed
in the United States and elsewhere, with recommendations and statistics.
Arranged by subject. Subject list in binder.

REPORTS ON ADMINISTRATION OF MILITARY JUSTICE IN EUROPEAN COUNTRIES. 1918-20. 6 ft. 6 in.   28

Correspondence, work papers, and reports of Col. W. C. Rigby resulting from a study of the administration of military justice in Belgium, France, Great Britain, and other countries. Colonel Rigby was chairman of a special mission sent to Europe in 1919 by the Secretary of War to study military jurisprudence. Arranged alphabetically by country investigated.

NOTATIONS OF CHANGES IN ARMY REGULATIONS. 1904-13. 2 ft. 6 in.   29

Card file used in connection with work on revisions of the manual, showing changes made in Army Regulations. Arranged numerically by paragraphs of Army Regulations.

SUGGESTIONS FOR REVISIONS OF THE COURT-MARTIAL MANUAL. 1919-21. 5 ft.   30

Card file containing suggested changes in the wording of the court-martial manual citing the paragraph of the pertinent Army Regulations, suggestion number, and name of person making suggestion. Arranged numerically by number of paragraph of Court-Martial Manual.

BRIEFS OF AEF COURT-MARTIAL CASES. 1918-20. 4 ft. 6 in.   31

Two card files containing briefs of American Expeditionary Forces court-martial cases, with citations to the cases. Arranged alphabetically by subject.

TESTIMONY CONCERNING COURT-MARTIAL PROCEDURE IN THE AEF. April 1920.
6 in.   32

Typed transcript of testimony of Brig. Gen. William W. Harts before the House of Representatives Select Committee on Expenditures in the War Department concerning the severity of court-martial sentences and the treatment of prisoners in the American Expeditionary Forces. Arranged chronologically.

Records of Investigations

REPORTS ON THE ORDER OF AMERICAN KNIGHTS. 1864. 1 ft.   33

Testimony, reports, and correspondence regarding the investigation by the Provost Marshal, Department of Missouri, of the activities of this secret order. Arranged chronologically.

REPORTS ON CONFEDERATE SUSPECTS. 1864-70. 3 vols. 9 in.   34

Copies of letters sent by Maj. L. C. Turner to the Secretary of War, Provost Marshal General, and others relating to persons suspected of having favored the Confederacy, and a few copies of letters of Judge Advocate General Joseph Holt, 1869-70, regarding correspondence by Major Turner. Arranged chronologically. Index in each volume arranged by name of correspondent.

RECORDS RELATING TO LINCOLN ASSASSINATION SUSPECTS. April 1865. 2 ft.   35

Correspondence, reports, and testimony of persons connected with the Lincoln assassination trial. Arranged alphabetically by initial letter of surname of the accused person. Many of these letters are abstracted in the register described below.

REGISTER OF RECORDS RELATING TO LINCOLN ASSASSINATION SUSPECTS ("Military
Commission Record Book"). 1865. 1 vol. 2 in.   36
Abstracts of letters, testimony, and reports regarding persons who
were in any way suspected in connection with the assassination of
President Lincoln. This material is supplementary to the military com-
mission case papers, MM 3951, filed in the series of court-martial case
papers (see entry 15). Arranged chronologically by date of receipt.
Name index in volume.

REGISTER OF LETTERS RECEIVED BY COL. H. L. BURNETT. April-August 1865.
1 vol. 2 in.   37
Abstracts of correspondence received by or referred to Col. H. L.
Burnett, Judge Advocate, who was assigned to investigate the assassination of President Lincoln. The name of the writer, the number assigned
the letter, the date, and notation of action taken are given. Arranged
chronologically. Index in volume. The correspondence registered in
this volume has not been found.

ENDORSEMENT BOOK OF COL. H. L. BURNETT RELATING TO LINCOLN ASSASSINA-
TION SUSPECTS. April-June 1865. 1 vol. 2 in.   38
Copies of endorsements by Colonel Burnett, with abstracts of
letters to which they relate, names of writers, and dates of letters
and endorsements. Arranged chronologically.

PAXTON HIBBEN CASE RECORDS. 1923-26. 2 ft.   39
Proceedings, exhibits, and correspondence relating to the work of
the Board composed of reserve officers that investigated the fitness
of Capt. Paxton Hibben to continue service as a reserve officer.
Arranged chronologically.

WILLIAM MITCHELL CASE RECORDS. 1925. 2 ft.   40
Photostatic and carbon copies of correspondence, exhibits, and
minutes of meetings of the Board of Aviation Inquiry, and work papers
of the Board relating to the trial by general court martial of Col.
William Mitchell, Air Service. These papers supplement the court-
martial case papers, which have been retained in the Office of the
Judge Advocate General. Arranged numerically by exhibit number.

RECORDS RELATING TO THE MARTIN-MITCHELL CONTROVERSY. 1927. 6 in.   41
Testimony, reports, and work papers of Col. Grant T. Trent, Judge
Advocate General's Office, relating to the controversy between Judge
Guy V. Martin and District Attorney F. Edward Mitchell of the Panama
Canal Zone. Colonel Trent was ordered to make the investigation by
authority of a letter from the Secretary of War, August 29, 1927.
Arranged chronologically.

Personnel Records

PERSONNEL LISTS. 1877-97. 3 vols. 3 in.   42
Lists of officers and clerks on duty in the Office of the Judge
Advocate General, with notations of leave taken and changes in status.
Arranged chronologically by month.

CORRESPONDENCE RELATING TO CIVILIAN PERSONNEL. 1887-98. 1 vol. 1 in. 43
   Press copies of letters sent by Acting Judge Advocate General
G. Norman Lieber concerning civilian personnel in the Office. Arranged
chronologically.

OFFICE ORDERS. 1918-23. 6 in. 44
   File copies of orders relating to the internal administration of
the Office of the Judge Advocate General and to personnel. Arranged
numerically.

BIOGRAPHICAL QUESTIONNAIRES. 1919-20. 2 ft. 45
   Forms filled in by military personnel giving name, rank, date of
birth, education, professional and military service, and honors
received. Arranged alphabetically.

CORRESPONDENCE RELATING TO WAR RISK INSURANCE. 1918-19. 1 ft. 46
   Correspondence relating to the appointment of Judge Advocates to
handle War Risk Insurance in various Army posts, camps, and stations,
together with their weekly reports. Arranged numerically, thereunder
alphabetically by names of posts, camps, and stations.

RECORDS RELATING TO THE FRENCH AND CREARY RETIREMENT CASES. 1920-23.
   6 in. 47
   Work papers of the Office of the Judge Advocate General relating
to the cases argued before various courts in regard to the retirement
of two colonels of the Regular Army. Arranged chronologically.

International Claims Records

MEXICAN CLAIMS CASE FILES. 1914-36. 4 ft. 48
   Correspondence between the Office of the Judge Advocate General and
other bureaus of the War Department, the Department of State, and the
Agent of the United States of the General Claims Arbitration, United
States and Mexico, regarding claims of Mexican citizens arising from
General Pershing's "Punitive Expedition" (1916) and the landing at
Vera Cruz (1914), together with memorials and briefs of claims. These
relate to claims for property damage, loss, and death caused by the
presence of United States troops. Arranged numerically by Judge
Advocate General's Office case numbers 1-39.

RECORDS RELATING TO NETHERLANDS CLAIMS CASES. 1932-40. 1 ft. 6 in. 49
   Correspondence, reports, testimony, and related papers concerning
cases before the Netherlands Claims Commission, which was created in
the War Department in 1932 to hear and determine Netherlands claims
arising from purchases of ordnance matériel by the Army during World
War I. Col. Joseph I. McMullen, Judge Advocate General's Office, was
Chairman and the members included Assistant Attorney General Charles
B. Rugg and Assistant Secretary of State Harvey H. Bundy, with Col.
Earl McFarland, Ordnance Department, as Secretary, and Maj. George P.
Hill, Judge Advocate General's Office, as Legal Adviser. This is a
fragmentary file; most of the records of the Commission itself were
turned over to the Department of State in 1933. Arranged chronologically.

RECORDS OF THE OFFICE OF THE ASSISTANT JUDGE ADVOCATE GENERAL

Col. William M. Dunn was appointed Assistant Judge Advocate General in 1864, with headquarters at Louisville, Ky. until 1867. During this period records of courts martial and of military commissions in the military departments of the Ohio, the Tennessee, the Cumberland, the Missouri, Arkansas, and Kansas were submitted to him for review before being forwarded to the Judge Advocate General in Washington.

REGISTERS OF COURT-MARTIAL CASE FILES. 1864-67. 6 vols. 1 ft. 1 in.   50
   Registers of case files received by Colonel Dunn, giving date of receipt, names of defendants, description of charges and sentence, and date transmitted to the Judge Advocate General, with a résumé of action taken in each case. Arranged chronologically by date received. Volumes lettered A-F. For separate indexes see the following entry.

INDEX TO REGISTERS OF COURT-MARTIAL CASE FILES. 1865-67. 5 vols.
   4 in.   51
   Index to volumes B-F of series described above. Arranged alphabetically by name of defendant.

ENDORSEMENT BOOK. 1864-66. 1 vol. 1 in.   52
   Contains number of endorsement, date written, date received, name of writer, subject of correspondence, date forwarded, and to whom referred, with brief of endorsement and of subsequent action. Arranged alphabetically by initial letter of surname of correspondent and numerically thereunder.

RECORDS OF THE OFFICE OF THE ACTING JUDGE ADVOCATE GENERAL IN EUROPE

The Office of the Acting Judge Advocate General in Europe for the American Expeditionary Forces was a field office of the Office of the Judge Advocate General in Washington. It was established on January 17, 1918, began to function on March 7, 1918, and was closed on October 6, 1919. The Office was established in order to insure as little delay as possible in the execution of sentences resulting from general courts martial. It examined and reviewed all general court-martial cases in which sentences of death, dismissal, or dishonorable discharge were imposed and all military commission cases originating in the AEF. Records of the Judge Advocate General's Department, AEF, are a part of Record Group No. 120, Records of the American Expeditionary Forces.

DECIMAL CORRESPONDENCE FILE. 1918-19. 4 ft. 6 in.   53
   Correspondence of Brig. Gen. E. A. Kreger and Col. H. A. White and copies of orders and reports regarding the examination and review of general court-martial cases in which a sentence of death, dismissal, or dishonorable discharge was imposed, as well as of cases handled by military commissions. After action was taken the case papers were forwarded to the Judge Advocate General for filing and are among the court-martial case files described in entry 15. Arranged according to the War Department subject classification scheme.

CONFIDENTIAL DECIMAL CORRESPONDENCE FILE. 1918-19. 1 ft. 6 in.   54
    Confidential correspondence, reports, and related papers arranged
according to the War Department subject classification scheme.

LIST OF AEF COURT-MARTIAL CASES. 1918-19. 5 ft. 6 in.   55
    Cards arranged alphabetically by name of defendant, giving rank,
organization, notation of action, and dates on which the case was
reviewed and the papers forwarded to the Judge Advocate General.
The case papers are included in the series described in entry 15.

RECORDS OF THE MILITARY RESERVATION DIVISION

        In 1894 the Judge Advocate General was made custodian of original
deeds and other papers pertaining to title, lease, or sale of military
reservations and other lands by the War Department. The present Military
Reservation Division was created in 1942.

RESERVATION FILE. 1809-1942. 30 ft.   56
    Correspondence, legal instruments, maps, plans, and miscellaneous
papers relating to real estate no longer in the possession of the War
Department. Arranged alphabetically by state and thereunder by reservation. The records pertaining to military reservations that are still
in the possession of the War Department have been retained by the
Military Reservation Division.

RECORDS OF THE LITIGATION DIVISION AND PREDECESSOR UNITS

        The Litigation Division was established in 1942 to exercise super-
vision, insofar as the War Department is concerned, over litigation in
which the Department is involved and to maintain liaison with the Department of Justice in connection therewith. It inherited records from
predecessor units, including the Civil Affairs Section established in
1925.

CIVIL AFFAIRS SECTION CORRESPONDENCE. 1925-31. 6 in.   57
    Correspondence with The Attorney General and War Department bureaus
regarding cases tried in the United States Court of Claims. Arranged
chronologically.

CONGRESSIONAL CASE FILE. 1926-37. 6 in.   58
    Correspondence, chiefly with Members of Congress, and other records
of the Civil Affairs Section regarding the payment of claims to individuals authorized by private acts of Congress. Arranged numerically, case
nos. 1-17. The index to this series is in the Litigation Division.

COURT OF CLAIMS CASE FILE. 1925-42. 22 ft. 6 in.   59
    Records relating to claims cases involving the War Department decided by
the Court of Claims, including reports of hearings, exhibits pertaining
to cases, printed Court of Claims material, and correspondence of the
Division and its predecessors (including the Civil Affairs Section) with
reference to rulings and claims. Arranged alphabetically by name of
person or firm involved.

DISTRICT OF COLUMBIA SUPREME COURT CASE FILE. 1923-40. 2 ft.   <u>60</u>
    Records relating to cases tried in the Supreme Court of the District
of Columbia in which the War Department was a party, including correspondence of the Office of the Judge Advocate General with other War
Department bureaus and with other departments. Arranged alphabetically
by name of individual or firm involved.

RECORDS OF THE WAR TRANSACTIONS BOARD

    The War Transactions Board was created within the War Department by
direction of the President, February 20, 1923, to cooperate with the
Board of Survey of the Department of Justice. The two Boards operated
as the Joint Board of Survey on war transactions. Subcommittees, which
reported to the Joint Board, made investigations of frauds arising out
of war contracts. This action resulted in review of those cases that
the Government wished to have settled before the contracts became void.
Almost all work was completed in 1925. Col. John A. Hull, Executive
Secretary of the Board, became Judge Advocate General in 1924. The records described below remained in the Office of the Judge Advocate General
until their transfer to the National Archives.

MINUTES OF MEETINGS OF THE JOINT BOARD. 1923-25. 1 binder. 2 in.   <u>61</u>
    Minutes kept by Col. John A. Hull, Executive Secretary, giving date
and place of meeting, members present, and a résumé of the proceedings.
Arranged chronologically.

CORRESPONDENCE. 1923-26. 2 ft.   <u>62</u>
    Correspondence, case files, reports, and related papers regarding the
legal review of contractual transactions of World War I in cooperation
with the Board of Survey of the Department of Justice. Arranged alphabetically under decimal classification number.

RECORDS OF THE INSULAR AFFAIRS SECTION

    In 1914 the Judge Advocate General took over the legal work formerly
handled by the Bureau of Insular Affairs of the War Department, and this
work was later centralized in the Insular Affairs Section of his Office.
The Section continued in existence until 1939, when the Bureau of Insular
Affairs was transferred from the War Department to the Department of the
Interior.

LEGAL OPINIONS. 1931-39. 7 binders. 6 in.   <u>63</u>
    Copies of memoranda to the Judge Advocate General and to the Chief of
the Bureau of Insular Affairs from the Chief of the Insular Affairs Section concerning legal matters arising from the administration of the
insular possessions of the United States. Arranged numerically, 1-406.

OFFICE DOCKETS. 1925-36. 3 binders. 3 in.   64
    Cards listing legal cases handled and giving the name of the court;
names of plaintiff and defendant; names of their attorneys; a notation
of pleadings indicating when they were due and filed; references to
proceedings; orders, rulings, and related correspondence; and notations
of action by the courts. Arranged numerically by case number.

OFFICE FILE. 1920-34. 2 ft.   65
    Papers of Col. W. C. Rigby, Chief of the Section, and reports,
memoranda, correspondence, and other material relating to cases of in-
terest to the Section. Arranged alphabetically by subject.

PUERTO RICAN CASE FILES. 1915-34. 10 ft. 6 in.   66
    Correspondence, briefs, testimony, and reports regarding cases before
the United States Circuit Court and the Supreme Court involving residents
of Puerto Rico. Arranged alphabetically by name of defendant.

PHILIPPINE CASE FILES. 1915-33. 3 ft.   67
    Correspondence, briefs, testimony, and reports regarding cases before
United States courts involving residents of the Philippines. Arranged
alphabetically by name of defendant.

INSULAR CASE RECORDS. 1918-32. 5 ft.   68
    Printed copies of records of cases tried before the United States
Circuit Court of Appeals and the United States Supreme Court involving
individuals and companies in Puerto Rico and the Philippine Islands
(incomplete file). Arranged chronologically and by court before which
tried.

RECORDS OF THE CENTRAL PATENT SECTION AND RELATED AGENCIES

    The Central Patent Section in the Office of the Judge Advocate Gen-
eral was created on July 11, 1921, as the successor to the activities of
the Central Patent Section, Supply Division, General Staff, which had
inherited various War Department records relating to patents upon its establishment on February 10, 1921, for "the control and coordination of
all patent activities of the Army and as a liaison with other governmen-
tal activities and departments."

    The records listed below are (1) records of various offices and
boards that were transferred with the related functions to the Central
Patent Section, (2) records created by the Section itself, and (3) foreign
claims records created by the Section and by the Commissions for Adjustment of Foreign Claims and of British Claims. As in many cases action
begun in one office was continued in one or more other offices, a number
of the series are closely related. Other records relating to patents are
in the Office of the Judge Advocate General.

Patent Section of the Supply Branch of the Purchase, Storage
and Traffic Division, War Department General Staff

This Section was organized in January 1919 to handle matters relating to the use of patented articles by the War Department and to the rights of War Department employees to patents on their inventions. It worked closely with the Munitions Patent Board.

DECIMAL CORRESPONDENCE FILE. 1919-20. 5 ft.   69
    Correspondence relating to the use of patented articles by the Government, to royalties, and to the infringement, assignment, and copyright of patents. Arranged by decimal number and alphabetically thereunder. For index see following entry.

INDEX TO DECIMAL CORRESPONDENCE FILE. 1919-20. 1 binder. 1 in.   70
    An alphabetical list by name of person or subject, giving decimal file number; a numerical list of documents under each decimal number indicating subject; and miscellaneous personnel information. Arranged alphabetically and by decimal number.

PATENT CASE FILE ("Dead File"). 1919-21. 4 ft. 6 in.   71
    Correspondence relating to applications for and grants of patents, with accompanying photostats and exhibits. This correspondence, classified under the decimal number "070., Inventions," was removed from the series described in entry 69 and arranged, apparently by the Central Patent Section, alphabetically by name or subject and given case nos. 200-593. For index see following entry.

INDEX TO PATENT CASE FILE ("Dead File"). 1919-21. 4 in.   72
    Arranged by name of inventor or subject. Gives date of action by Munitions Patent Board, decimal file number, and "dead file" number.

RECORD OF ACTION ON PATENT CASES. 1919-21. 1 binder. 1 in.   73
    Record of action on specific cases, giving name of claimant, brief résumé of action, and dates of action and referral to the Interdepartmental Patents Board. Arranged by name of company. Index in volume.

AIR SERVICE CONTRACT REFERENCE FILE. 1919. 6 in.   74
    Work papers relating to possible patent claims involved in Air Service contracts made during World War I. Arranged numerically by contract number.

ADMINISTRATIVE REFERENCE FILE. 1919. 6 in.   75
    Bulletins, orders, circulars, and memoranda relating to patents and patented articles. Arranged chronologically.

PATENT INFORMATION SHEETS. 1919-20. 13 ft. 6 in.   76
    Reference sheets to contracts let by the War Department involving the use of patented materials, giving subject, number, and date of contract and the cost and use made of the patented material.

Munitions Patent Board

The Munitions Patent Board was established in September 1918 for the purpose of coordinating the policies of the War and Navy Departments in patent matters. Its membership included Thomas Ewing, Chairman; Max Thelen, War Department representative; and Pickens Neagle, Navy Department representative. The Board considered questions regarding all phases of patent matters brought before it by the War and Navy Department members. It ceased to function in 1921.

PATENT CASE FILE ("Dead File"). 1918-21. 2 ft. 6 in.   77
    Correspondence of the Board, copies of patents, and reports on the decisions of the Board on applications for and claims to patents, including copies of minutes and miscellaneous correspondence with the Patent Section of the War Department Claims Board. Arranged (apparently by the Central Patent Section) alphabetically by subject or name and given case nos. 594-686. (See also entry 71.)

INDEX TO PATENT CASE FILE ("Dead File"). 1918-21. 1 binder. 1 in.   78
    Arranged by name of inventor. Gives date of action by Munitions Patent Board, decimal file number, and "dead file" number.

Central Patent Section of the Supply Division, War Department General Staff

DAILY DIARY. 1921. 1 binder. 1 in.   79
    Informal notes on conferences of officials of the Section and notations concerning personnel. Arranged chronologically.

Patents Branch of the Procurement Division, Office of the Chief of Ordnance

The Patents Branch was organized in March 1918 within the Procurement Division of the Office of the Chief of Ordnance and was concerned with ordnance patents and inventions, contracts concerning patent rights, and payments of royalities and other fees. In January 1919 the Office was divided, and the functions and personnel having to do with contract matters and payment of compensation for the use of inventions were transferred to the Patent Section of the Purchase, Storage and Traffic Division. Maj. Amasa M. Holcombe, Chief of the Section, was made the War Department representative on the Munitions Patent Board.

OFFICE FILE OF MAJOR HOLCOMBE. 1917-19. 1 ft.   80
    Correspondence of Maj. A. M. Holcombe, Chief of the Section, relating to personnel and to ordnance patent matters and copies of patents. Arranged alphabetically by person or subject.

ORDNANCE CONTRACT PATENTS LIST. 1918-19. 1 ft. 6 in.   <u>81</u>
    A list of ordnance contracts, giving contract number, subject, and patent rights, if any, involved. Arranged numerically.

ORDNANCE SPECIFICATIONS FOR BIDDERS. 1917-19. 6 in.   <u>82</u>
    Printed and mimeographed ordnance specifications for bidders. Arranged by ordnance document number.

ORDNANCE MATÉRIEL FILE. 1919. 1 ft.   <u>83</u>
    Photostat copies of drawings of ordnance equipment. Arranged numerically by number of ordnance drawing.

INDEX TO ORDNANCE CONTRACTS. 1917-19. 26 binders. 2 ft. 6 in.   <u>84</u>
    Index to contracts in contract file of the Office of the Chief of Ordnance (in Record Group No. 156) in the National Archives. Contains information regarding patent rights, if any, involved in ordnance contracts. Arranged alphabetically by symbol of procuring division and numerically thereunder.

PATENTS FILE. 1918-19. 2 ft.   <u>85</u>
    Correspondence relating to the investigation of infringement of ordnance patents, together with copies of patents. Arranged by name of inventor.

Interdepartmental Patents Board

    The Interdepartmental Patents Board was created by President Harding on August 9, 1922, to make a comprehensive study of policies concerning the patent rights of Government employees with regard to their inventions. Col. Joseph I. McMullen, Chief of the Patent Section, was the War Department member and Secretary until the Board was abolished in 1933.

CHAIRMAN'S CORRESPONDENCE. 1922-23. 1 ft. 6 in.   <u>86</u>
    Correspondence of Dr. Andrew Stewart of the Department of the Interior, Chairman of the Board, with Government bureaus regarding the patent rights of their employees. Includes exhibits and related materials. Arranged numerically. Numerical list at beginning of file.

SECRETARY'S CORRESPONDENCE AND BOARD MINUTES. 1922-23. 6 in.   <u>87</u>
    Correspondence of Colonel McMullen with War Department bureaus and other Government agencies and copies of minutes of meetings of the Board. Arranged chronologically.

Central Patent Section

Records Relating to Domestic Patents

PATENT CASE FILE ("Dead File"). 1921-40. 25 ft.   88
   Correspondence regarding applications for and grants of patents;
photostats of patents and other materials; and exhibits relating to
specific cases. Arranged alphabetically and numerically by case, nos.
1-799. Indexed in the general index in the Patents Division, Office
of the Judge Advocate General.

COURT OF CLAIMS CASE FILE. 1921-42. 68 ft.   89
   Correspondence of the Office of the Judge Advocate General with
other War Department bureaus and the Department of Justice regarding
the defense of suits brought in the Court of Claims alleging infringe-
ment of patents by the War Department. This correspondence relates
only to completed cases; that relating to cases still pending remains
in the Office of the Judge Advocate General. Arranged numerically by
Judge Advocate General case number. Index is in the Patents Division,
Office of the Judge Advocate General.

HISTORICAL FILE. 1917-40. 12 ft. 6 in.   90
   Case papers considered of historical value by the Central Patent
Section and relating to various types of patent matters under consider-
ation by the Section. Arranged numerically by file numbers 1-134. The
index to the file and a few case papers that belong in it remain in the
Patents Division, Office of the Judge Advocate General.

REGISTER OF CORRESPONDENCE. 1924-26. 1 binder. 1 in.   91
   Abstracts of correspondence, giving date received, name of correspondent, nature of request, and action taken. Arranged chronologically.

MUSCLE SHOALS CORRESPONDENCE FILE. 1918-34. 11 ft.   92
   Correspondence with the Office of the Chief of Ordnance and other
War Department bureaus, the Department of Justice, and Congress concerning proposed legislation with regard to Muscle Shoals, together
with work papers, blueprints, and related materials. Arranged
alphabetically by subject and chronologically thereunder.

INDEX TO MUSCLE SHOALS CORRESPONDENCE FILE. 1930-32. 1 ft. 2 in. 93
   Arranged by names of correspondent. Gives date of letter, résumé
of subject, and file number.

LIST OF INVENTORS IN THE FIELD OF ELECTRICITY. 1907-31. 4 in.   94
   Cards giving inventor's name, patent number, patent subject, date
of expiration of patent, and company holding patent rights. Arranged
by name of inventor.

PHOTOSTATS OF PATENTS. 1913-26. 2 ft. 6 in.   95
   Photostat copies of various patents used as a reference file.
Arranged by name of inventor.

Records Relating to German-Austrian Patent Claims

The Settlement of War Claims Act, passed by Congress on March 10, 1928, provided for the appointment of a War Claims Arbiter and directed other agencies of the Government to furnish him with the records and information needed as well as to detail personnel to assist him. The following are records resulting from assistance rendered by the War Department in connection with the settlement of claims in which it was concerned.[1] The work was performed by a group in the Central Patent Section.

ADMINISTRATIVE FILE. 1928-33. 15 ft.   96
    Executive and office orders, valuation analyses, office and investigators' reports, reports to the Department of Justice, reports of Col. Hugh C. Smith's European trip, personnel papers, the War Claims Arbiter's reports, administrative orders, dockets, opinions, minutes, and correspondence. Arranged by subject.

CASE FILE. 1928-31. 133 ft.   97
    Briefs, exhibits, correspondence, and decisions. Arranged by case number and thereunder by patent number. For indexes see following entry.

INDEXES TO CASE FILES. 1928-31. 8 ft. 3 in.   98
    Five card indexes, one arranged alphabetically by name of claimant, two by case number, and two alphabetically by the subject of the patent.

REGISTER OF CASES FILED. 1929-31. 2 binders. 4 in.   99
    Gives case and docket numbers, date of filing of the case, the patents involved in the case, and the action taken. Arranged by case, nos. 1-1072.

RECORD OF STATUS OF CASES. 1928-31. 4 binders. 4 in.   100
    List of cases before the War Claims Arbiter giving claimant, his attorney, and action taken. Arranged by docket numbers, 1-1180.

PATENTS FILE. 1900-1917. 8 ft.   101
    Printed copies of United States patents granted to Germans and Austrians prior to the first World War. Arranged by subject of patent and thereunder by patent number.

FOREIGN PATENTS FILE. 1879-1927. 6 ft. 6 in.   102
    Photostats of German, Austrian, and other foreign patents involved in claims. Arranged alphabetically by country and thereunder numerically by patent number.

---

[1] See also "Preliminary Checklist of War Department Foreign Patents Claims Records, 1922-33," compiled by Stuart Portner, Victor Gondos, Jr., and Henry H. Eddy (Sept. 1943). For an account of records of the Department of Justice see the "Preliminary Checklist of the Records of the Claims Division of the Department of Justice, 1928-1931, Relating to the Defense of Patent Claims Before the War Claims Arbiter Under the Settlement of War Claims Act of 1928," compiled by F. Hardee Allen and Thayer Boardman (June 1945).

LIST OF PATENTS. 1928-30. 1 ft.   103
   Card file giving patent group number and case number (see entry 97)
and indicating the date sent to the Department of Justice. Arranged by
patent number.

LISTS OF PATENTS. 1900-1930. 7 ft. 6 in.   104
   Four card lists of patents giving inventor, subject and number of
patent, and date granted. Two lists arranged by patent number, one by
name of inventor, and one by War Department Bureau and by patent number
thereunder.

LIST OF RADIO PATENTS. 1898-1931. 4 in.   105
   Card list giving subject of patent, its number, inventor, and date
granted. Arranged alphabetically by subject.

LISTS OF PATENT ASSIGNMENTS. 1900-1921. 2 ft. 3 in.   106
   Three card lists giving subject of patent, patent number, date granted,
name of the patentee, and the firm to which the patent was assigned. Two
lists arranged alphabetically by subject, one numerically.

LISTS OF PATENTS ASSIGNED TO THE CHEMICAL FOUNDATION. 1900-1922. 3 ft.
      3 in.   107
   Two card files giving name of patentee, number of patent, and date
granted. Arranged by patent number.

LIST OF PATENTS SEIZED BY THE ALIEN PROPERTY CUSTODIAN. 1900-1920.
      1 ft.   108
   List of seized patents that were licensed, sold, returned to former
owners, or held by the Alien Property Custodian, giving patent number,
date issued, inventor, and subject of patent. Arranged by type of action
and by patent number thereunder.

LIST OF APPLICATIONS FOR SEIZED PATENTS. 1918-20. 2 vols. 4 in.   109
   List of applications for patents seized by the Alien Property Custo-
dian giving trust number, date of seizure, disposition, and assignee.
Arranged by patent number.

PATENT APPLICATION LIST. 1915-24. 4 ft.   110
   Card list of patents that were applied for and granted, giving person
to whom assigned, patent number or application number, patentee, subject
of patent, and date of application. Arranged by patent number.

VALIDITY AND VALUATION REPORTS. 1928-31. 2 ft.   111
   Reports on the validity and valuation of patents involved in cases
before the War Claims Arbiter and on the disposition of the cases. Arranged by subject.

LISTS OF VALIDITY AND VALUATION REPORTS. 1928-31. 1 ft. 2 in.   112
   Two card files giving patent and case numbers, notations of investiga-
tion, and date the information was forwarded to the Department of Justice.
(See entries 97 and 111.) Arranged by patent number.

LIST OF EXPERTS. 1928-30. 6 in.   113
    Card file listing experts, giving date assigned to investigate case,
type of case, and case and patent numbers. Arranged by name of expert.

OFFICE FILE OF MARK A. WOODELL, SPECIAL INVESTIGATOR. 1928-31. 2 ft. 114
    Printed copies of patents and related papers. Arranged alphabetically
by subject.

OFFICE FILE OF SIMON KLOSKY, SPECIAL INVESTIGATOR. 1928-31. 1 ft.
      6 in.   115
    Printed copies of patents and other material relating principally to
dyes and synthetic rubber. Arranged alphabetically by subject.

LIST OF COMMERCIAL FIRMS. 1928-30. 4 in.   116
    Card list of American companies mentioned in case papers (see entry
97), containing company name and address, case number, patent number
involved in case, subject of case, and name of War Department bureau
interested in the case. Arranged alphabetically by name of firm.

LISTS OF INVENTORS. 1929-31. 4 ft. 6 in.   117
    Three card files giving name of inventor, subject and serial number
of patent, and date issued. Arranged alphabetically by name of inventor.

REGISTER OF CLAIMS. 1919-31. 1 ft.   118
    Gives number of patent, date of seizure, owner, disposition, name of
licensee, purchaser, to whom released, and amount received from sale or
license. Arranged numerically by case number.

DOCKET BOOK OF CLAIMS. 1928-31. 1 binder. 2 in.   119
    Memoranda of requests made for reports from the Alien Property Custo-
dian on patents, 1900-17, giving docket and case numbers, assignee, and
patents involved. Arranged by docket number.

GERMAN-AUSTRIAN TRADEMARK INDEX. 1928-31. 4 in.   120
    Card file giving name of trademark, case (see entry 97) and docket
numbers, and date of action by the War Claims Arbiter. Arranged alphabetically by name of trademark.

Commission for Adjustment of Foreign Claims

    This Commission was created by War Department general orders of
February 28, 1922, "to hear and determine all questions of performance
or non-performance, arising out of the agreement known as the 'Bolling
Agreement' of June 1917, and such other matters relating to foreign
claims as may from time to time be assigned to it by the Secretary of
War." It was dissolved June 26, 1924. For a detailed account of its
history and work see "Preliminary Checklist of War Department Foreign
Patent Claims Records, 1922-1933," compiled by Stuart Portner, Victor
Gondos, Jr., and Henry H. Eddy.

ADMINISTRATIVE FILE. 1922-24. 2 ft. <u>121</u>
Correspondence on the administration of the Commission. Arranged chronologically.

CLAIMS CASE FILES. 1922-24. 18 ft. <u>122</u>
Transcripts of hearings, exhibits, testimonials, briefs, and related papers. Arranged by case, nos. 1-40.

EXHIBITS. 1922-24. 16 ft. 6 in. <u>123</u>
Blueprints, drawings, charts, photostats, and photographs. Arranged by case number.

AERONAUTICAL PATENTS REFERENCE FILE. 1919-24. 5 ft. 6 in. <u>124</u>
Copies of American aeronautical patents. Arranged by class and sub-class and numerically thereunder. For index see following entry.

AERONAUTICAL PATENTS REFERENCE FILE INDEX. 1919-24. 1 binder.
6 in. <u>125</u>
Gives number of patent, name of inventor, subject of invention, and numbers of expired patents. Arranged by class and sub-class and numerically thereunder.

Commission for Adjustment of British Claims

This Commission was established by letter of The Adjutant General, War Department, dated July 7, 1932. Its final report was submitted and approved February 11, 1933. For a detailed account of the Commission's work see the "Preliminary Checklist of War Department Foreign Patents Claims Records," referred to above.

FILE OF THE CHAIRMAN. 1917-34. 6 in. <u>126</u>
Correspondence of Col. Joseph I. McMullen, Chairman, 1932-34, with reference materials on previous patent acts, negotiations, and agreements, 1917-33. Arranged alphabetically by subject.

INDEX TO FILE OF THE CHAIRMAN. 1923-34. 2 in. <u>127</u>
Contains subject résumé of correspondence, date received, and the number under which the correspondence is filed. Arranged alphabetically by subject.

GENERAL ADMINISTRATIVE FILE. 1932-34. 6 in. <u>128</u>
Includes travel vouchers, time and pay reports, and personnel records. Arranged alphabetically by name of employee.

CASE FILE. 1932-33. 7 ft. <u>129</u>
Transcripts of hearings, briefs, testimonies, exhibits, and related papers of cases heard by the Commission. Arranged by case, nos. 1-17.

"NEW CLAIMS" FILE. 1932-33. 6 in. <u>130</u>
Correspondence relating to claims made after the establishment of the Commission. Arranged alphabetically by name of claimant.

www.ingramcontent.com/pod-product-compliance
Lightning Source LLC
Chambersburg PA
CBHW081423270326

41931CB00015B/3386